THE SEASON OF FLESH

By BYRON HERBERT REECE

Poetry

THE BALLAD OF THE BONES

BOW DOWN IN JERICHO

A SONG OF JOY

THE SEASON OF FLESH

Fiction

BETTER A DINNER OF HERBS

E·P·DUTTON & CO. INC

1852 1955

CREATIVE · 103 YEARS · PUBLISHING

The Season of Flesh

BY

BYRON HERBERT REECE

E. P. DUTTON & COMPANY, INC.
New York, 1955

Copyright 1955, by E. P. Dutton & Co., Inc.
All rights reserved. Printed in the U. S. A.

FIRST EDITION

¶ No part of this book may be reproduced
in any form without permission in writing
from the publisher, except by a reviewer
who wishes to quote brief passages in con-
nection with a review written for inclusion in
magazine or newspaper or radio broadcast.

ACKNOWLEDGMENT AND COPYRIGHT DATES OF
INDIVIDUAL POEMS:

AMERICAN WEAVE: *As Mary Was Awalking,
A Platitude of Plato*, 1952; *The Altitudes of
Love*, XVIII, No. 1. 1953.

THE FAWNLIGHT: *The Barrier*, 1953.

THE GEORGIA REVIEW: *The Poet and the Ves-
tures*, 1952; *The Perception of Age*, 1953;
In The Corridor, 1954.

KALEIDOGRAPH: *The Stay-At-Home, The Gift-
ing*, 1952; *The Fallen Snow, I'll Make My
Love A Present as The Exchange*, 1953.

OLIVANT QUARTERLY: *The Disparates, At
Autumn Things Are All at Odds*, 1953.

POETRY CHAP-BOOK: *Encounter, The Dark
and the Light*, 1953.

POETRY DIGEST: *The Bethrothed from the
Grave*, 1954.

THE PROGRESSIVE FARMER: *Spring Orchards*,
1954.

THE CHESTATEE: *Jonathan in Jeopardy*, 1952.

THE LAND: *The Laboring Man*, 1952; *Spring
Song, A Fire of Boughs, Time and the Cherry
Tree*, 1953.

THE LYRIC: *Astronomics, The Fallow*, 1953;
In Absence, 1954.

35989 LIBRARY OF CONGRESS CATALOG CARD NUMBER: 55-5362

For

BARRY WILLIAMS

TABLE OF CONTENTS

CONTENTS

CONTENTS

III

IV

[9]

CONTENTS

THE SEASON OF FLESH

IN THE CORRIDOR

Clouds I remember, a day all dull and dun;
The sun may have shone at the first for a little space,
I do not remember. Clouds I remember, and one
Figure departing, one grave unsmiling face.

The voice reading ceased at the sound of the bell
And I closed the ponderous book on Herrick's song,
Caught still in the youthful music, caught in the spell
Of its sound on a youthful tongue.

The door of that classroom fronts on an open hall
And one may go by the way he came, or not;
But this was the eve of holiday for all
And from my desk I followed the laughing lot.

Just where the hallway opens upon the street
One looked back for a moment, as if to find
Whether my gaze sought his, and, should they meet,
Whether my mind

Was still for the ageless music of Herrick, or
For the aging day, or the book,
Or for the face at the end of the corridor
And its fleeting backward look.

I

THE BETROTHED FROM THE GRAVE*

The night crept dark to Margaret's door,
Within her bower she sat
And sewed a seam by candle gleam;
Sweet William knocked thereat.

Yet he was changed from him that stood
And knocked upon her door
As lover oathed to his betrothed,
For he drew breath no more.

Sweet William stood a livid ghost
New-come from graveyard ground.
Long he had slept, yet when she wept
He wakened to the sound.

When Margaret wept sweet William woke
Drear in his dread abode,
The dark grave rent, to Margaret went
With his coffin for a load.

When he had reached her bower door
He tirled at the pin,
And Margaret heard his knock and stirred
But would not let him in.

"Oh, art thou come from graveyard ground,
And art thou come by stealth
As oft before to my bower door?
If thou be sprite of health

* Cf. headnote Child Ballad no. 77

"And well to greet the name repeat
  Of Him that died on Tree."
And, "Jesus Christ," the ghost said twict,
  And wide the door flung she.

"How is it in the grave?" she said
  When she had let him in.
Said he, "I wis, like heaven's bliss,"
  And kissed her cheek and chin.

"Then I shall follow to the grave
  If all therein be well."
"Ah, no," said he, "for verily
  It is like blackest hell."

"If it be hell I weep thee well
  And may not cease to weep,"
Said Margaret fair, combing his hair
  Danked in the grave's damp keep.

"Forbid, my dear, the ready tear,
  Let not thy grief down flood,
For when you weep my coffin deep
  Is filled with lappered blood.

"If thou forbid," Sweet William said,
"The brimming tear to fall
  Then it is well, and then not hell
  To lie wrapped up in pall.

"And sigh not, dear, each sigh I hear,
  But sing, for at thy song
  Like gardens green the grave within
  With the rose-leaf is hung."

Hour by dark hour, beyont her bower,
The swifting night was sped.
Upon the stroke of midnight spoke
The black cock and the red.

Upon the stroke of midnight spoke
The white cock from the post:
'Tis time and past that thou must haste
To kirk and lay thy ghost.

"I must away!" sweet William cried
When all the cocks had crown,
And wearily with his coffin he
Back to the grave was gone.

Long was the way; it was near day
When they to kirk had come,
For Margaret, lamenting yet,
Followed him to the tomb.

"Haste home, fair Margaret," he said,
"And never weep me more
Lest thou should flood my grave with blood,
As I told thee before.

"Oh, haste home, Margaret," he said,
"And never weep me more
That rose may bloom within my tomb,
As I told thee before."

Sweet William's cheek blanched white from rose
And all his yellow hair
As in a spell like dead leaves fell
Till his skull bone was bare.

"The night is going, Margaret,
Look, look up at the sky!"
While Margaret stared the gray ghost fared
Lone in the grave to lie.

Sighing or singing in her bower
Fair Margaret sewed alone
Until death came and graved her name
With William's on the stone.

His room betimes was drenched with blood,
Betimes, if she had sung,
Like gardens green his grave within
With the rose-leaf was hung.

.

JONATHAN IN JEOPARDY

I Samuel, 14

When Jonathan fought at Michmash
Hunger troubled his tongue;
As he saw the light from their broad swords flash
And heard the Philistine armor clash
He dreamed of the taste of honey
And the sound of the wild bee's song.

Where Jonathan slew twenty
Of the enemies of God
In the woods was honey in plenty;
The people ate not any
Because of an oath, but Jonathan
To the honey touched his rod

And the rod was covered with honey
And Jonathan did eat.
Then a soldier said: Thy father, he
Charged us swear that verily
Till the Philistines felt his vengeance
This day we should touch no meat.

Then Jonathan spoke lightly
And said: Behold, mine eyes
Are opened so that I truly see
Because of the sweet I ate. Said he:
Eat of the spoils of thy slaughter
And the eating shall make thee wise.

For, see, if ye had eaten
Of the spoils of the enemy
Thy enterprise to sweeten

The more had they been beaten,
For the hand made free for looting
For one had slaughtered three!

Then the people fell to feasting
And ate both flesh and blood;
And that was but a little thing,
But for the vow's transgressing
At the King's son's instigation
In jeopardy Jonathan stood.

For the lot fell upon Jonathan
That searched them all of guilt.
And King Saul said: What hast thou done?
And straightway answered him his son:
I hungered and ate of the honey
That from the hives was spilt.

Then King Saul looked on Jonathan
With a wild and baleful eye,
And he said: If thou wert twice my son
Yet for the evil thou hast done,
For the sweet taste of transgression
Know thou shouldst surely die!

But the people cried to King Saul
His murderous hand to halt:
Shall he that wrought more than us all
This day, for one transgression fall?
Shall the King's son lose his honor
And die for a single fault?

And the people saved the king's son;
And henceforth when he ate

He thought of his own transgression
And of their intercession
And never again when feasting
Was honey upon his plate.

MEG

Meg goes not so merrily
As any need despise,
Verily, not merrily
As at the moon's demise.
No one yet has found the boot
With which she trod the skies.

The horn has shrunk to hang-again
That fleshed upon the hunt.
No dew was tattle in the corn
Of where the quarry went.
Now Meg abides her chatter-bones
And doesn't wish to stir.
For that's Proserpine who brings
A mated shoe to her.

And Meg goes not so merrily
As any need to think
Her happiness a straw to flay
Could they but find the stick.
It is a gulf too deep to brink
Between the lost and found.
However hard the iron is struck
Its bell is not the bond.
Poor Meg.

II

THE DISPARATES

That whisper in my marrowbone,
As I wake at night,
Falls on the ear of stone
Once cupped to the quiet

Breathing of centuries
Passed away,
Their tremulous queries
Quiet as they.

Hiding its natal heat
Too deep to guess,
In silence stone hears repeat
For emphasis

Whisperer his whisper
Passing away,
Stirs not at his anguished stir,
Says no doubts nay.

Itself, till summer's gone,
Vine and leaf enmesh;
So wears its brother bone
The season of flesh.

ASTRONOMICS

We dwell, not strangers to the earth
But intimates of spheres
That constellate around a hearth
But solitary bears

Each its equal progeny,
Its populating one
The circuit set for solar day
By its elected sun.

While passing planetary here
Fortunate they are
Proficient as astronomer
To gauge a single star

And fathom how benign its air,
How mild its zones, and then
By implication, as it were,
Deduce the citizen.

THE DARK AND THE LIGHT

Each thing woken into light
Is of darkness, and it goes
Hence into its native night;
Yet the sun has shaped the rose.

Nothing of its genesis
Bears true testament: the vine's
Tendril thrust through darkness is
Rooted where all creation shines.

THE FALLOW

The heart's true heights of granite
Silt downward in the flow
Of time to spread a fallow
Where seeds take root and grow.

There spring the scattered seedlings
And soon each rapid shoot
Bears: Love its tender blossoms,
And wrath its bitter fruit.

THE TASTE OF FRUIT

That incidence,
That root of once,
With honeydew was filled;
Let naught abate
But reason wait
And I will bring a child.

The dreaded claw
Was not the law
Nor red which terror wrought;
But trust the ear
And we will hear
How the child was taught:

The taste of fruit
Was never sweet
As played upon the harp.
But at expense
Of innocence
It was an elder spoke.

ENCOUNTER

As I met early
A gray old man,
I with nearly
All life to span,

And he but a candle
This side of dusk,
His sage's mantle
Seemed suddenly husk.

PAST INNOCENCE

The stillness makes a myth of air
Explicit as a word,
And it is only children there
Who play as they afford;

Then shift. But O we long to keep
And know it will not stay,
That drift past innocence and sleep
And all their rags away.

NECESSARY LIGHT

Clear is the shadow in his eye
Who fronts a sun of strange degree.
Had reason thought to come this way,
Or found it, logic, blond as he,

Had sunned the other side the wall
And learned in necessary light
How random set are stones that fall
To liberate, grope-touched by night.

THE CYCLE

That which is carnal to its source,
Before the chill and spade,
Turns, dreaming crooked intercourse
In nude Susanna's glade.

But poison prospers and appalls
Where never wed the ring.
The asp by monastery walls
Goes careful of his fang.

THE COUNTRY GUEST

The guise is innocence and hurt
And hearty at the core;
The ratio is bereavement
To hope of native air.

No country foot may step exempt
That no unmeasured mile
But pages gossip their contempt
In corridors of tile.

THE STAY-AT-HOME

The fields of Hughly held him,
The land where he was born.
With fence to mend and cows to tend
And care of wheat and corn
He had no lief to wander
Beyond his place of birth,
But often he would ponder
The luring lands of earth.

He loved the fields of Hughly
And every hill that stood
To bind him in with other men
Like him in bone and blood,
Who often thought of going
But had the will to stay
And turn them to their hoeing
When cocks crew up the day.

Yet, as the gypsy-hearted
Hearken when distance sings,
The sounds he most regarded
Were all of passing things:
Swift waters flowing,
Winds to westward blowing,
Footsteps outward going
And wild, wandering wings.

FIDUS ACHATES

Sorrow's like a little death
Not yet grown to fatal stature,
Yet no menace to the breath
Grows of Sorrow's gentle nature.

Joy withers with the years
Ending youth, which is an instant;
Sorrow with her store of tears
Is by nature full and constant.

Never choose between the two:
Joy, parting, will commend you
To her sister Sorrow, true
Through all trouble, to befriend you.

I'LL MAKE MY LOVE A PRESENT

I'll make my love a present
Of lilacs dipped in dew,
A rosy wreath, a pheasant,
A preening peacock, too.

For every gaud of beauty
And every gift of grace
I give her out of duty
She'll spirit something base

Or niggard from my nature;
And when each blot is gone
Give me myself, each feature
Made faultless as her own.

MY TRUE-LOVE

Blacker than night is my True-Love's hair,
My True-Love's brow is bonny;
My True-Love's lips are ruby and fair
And touched with the taste of honey.

Whiter than milk is my True-Love's throat
That soars like a marble column
And bears a bell of marvelous note
With accents airy and solemn.

Tender and strong are my True-Love's hands,
Their strength by mercy made dearer;
Each five of fingers are fiercer than brands
And total a ten of terror.

Because it is dearer to breathe than breath
And low and more utter than loathing,
My love for my True-Love is darker than death
And whiter than Christ's own clothing.

I taste of the Wine from my True-Love's lips,
The Bread is my True-Love's body;
And the vinegar waits at my fingertips,
And the Cross stands hewn and ready.

THE ALTITUDES OF LOVE

If ever I saw my True-Love
Coming from Pindar Lake
And I in the Hughly Hills above
I'd hasten, for love's sake,

By the descending roadway;
We'd meet at middle height
Before the slant of the day
Tipped westward toward the night.

For it is not meet in darkness
In a low place to lie down;
Nor where the glow of love is less—
At the luminescent crown

Of a wild, wind-deafened summit—
Than the sun's that lights the bed.
Let the eunuch and the hermit
Mate with the lightless dead,

And the man that mocks the lightning
Love himself alone;
Let two to each their comfort bring
To a bed not wholly stone

And lie where leaves have dappled
The floor with light and shade
Since the two in the garden grappled
When first the world was made.

IN ABSENCE

I call in the cold and silence, I speak your name
And hear no answer but echo, and ache with grief.
Find me in fire, for love, in the flickering flame
Fed by fagot and leaf.

Whenever the rose lifts resolute in spring
Find me, for love, in each unfolding petal;
In the greening leaf, in every living thing
Know me a little.

Breathe me, for love, in breathing the common air;
Of spirit or matter, of all things find me part.
Greet me in absence, for love, for I am there;
And in your heart

Keep me, O Love, as near as the constant flood
Washing its chambers. Wear me, for warmth, as close
In the channels of ivory mazing your leaping blood
As your warm blood flows.

THE END OF LOVE

That I have ended a long love
Gives nothing cause to mourn;
So change your tune, you mourning dove
That calls in the still corn.

Now that I have foreshortened night
And put my sorrow by,
Frisk all your length, you long light
That tells the time of the sky.

The least of love is error,
To watch by a single door;
The most of love is terror—
But now I love no more

And comfort shall attend my dreams
And perfect peace prevail;
So dance and sing, you winding streams
That dapple in the dale.

A FAREWELL

A rainy wind blows from the south,
A sudden showering blinds the pane;
The mold shall whiten my True-Love's mouth
Ere it meet mine again.

THE DIVIDE

The face of one long loved in vain,
Unfashioned by the years
Into his native dust again,
The ransom of my tears

Redeemed from darkness. Straight he stood
With summons in his eyes
Beyond the wild weir and the wood
That warden paradise

From the assault of flesh with flood
To drown, and thorn to tear
Away the garment stitched with blood
Of any passing there.

Though he entreat my gaze from bliss
I reverence that divide
Until for raiment such as his
My flesh be put aside

And past the current nought can force
My soul trespass with ease,
And win as stopless in its course
As vapor through those trees.

TUNE ON AN OLD STRING
Played for the Beloved

Hey nonny no,
While the seas flow?
But seas flow ever;
While the winds blow?
But winds cease never;
What then should ail the song
And make us dance the measure wrong,
If the seas be not at fault
And the winds never halt?

Hey nonny no,
In their despite
From glim towers the watchers go
Blind into the night;
And the dancing foot
Casts its dancing boot
And wears instead
A shoe of lead.

Indeed, the change is wrought
In the high-domed house,
Home of dream and thought;
In the dancer's tower that leans
Till its length lie prone
And that footer of the greens
Be somewhere gone
Where are no seas to flow
Nor any winds to blow,
Hey nonny no!

AMONG THE HEADSTONES

Among these stones, but not to read,
Of Sundays youthful couples come;
Old lovers lying blind and dumb
Sleep as they pass and pay no heed.

THE BARRIER

In Elder's wood beyond the meadow's end
Nothing disturbs the quiet with speech but wind
In conversation with a nodding tree
Eager with his old crony to agree;

Or so it seems. Wind's speech is low or slurred
So syllables that else might make a word
Fail of distinction in the ear, or pass
A foreign language never learned, alas.

Sometimes when in a hostile frame of mind
And I suspect myself by wind maligned
I read accord with that old gossip meant
When the mute tree nods gravely in assent,

And wish one's banishment, the other's fall.
Beyond such barrier as divides us all
The wind may speak of other matters; true.
I'd not suspect that prattler if I knew.

FROM WINDOWS TOWARD THE LIGHTED WEST

From windows toward the lighted west
The rigid rays of sunlight, weighed
Beyond the fulcrum at the crest
Of the horizon, lift and fade.

And objects, all their purple gear
Richer than than robes of pomp and pride
Divested, reach for darkness; rear
Tall, tower and wall, their shadow-side,

While limned with aureoles of light
As silver-thin as shears could cut
The mountains emanate toward night
And rifted earth and sky grow shut.

And all is darkness. West the tide
Of light recedes from widening shores
And blackened beaches which divide
The ebb of day no sun restores

From day renewed in golden floes
Inflooding from the eastern rim
Of continents; and darkness goes
As luminescent runnels brim

Wide as the wash of ebon seas.
Then night is gone. And bone and breath
Stir to the pulse of such release
From that dark metaphor of death

As eastered in Jerusalem
When He that slept woke where He lay
To stare from that intensest tomb
Into the resurrected day.

BEREAVEMENT

Bereavement: It will come
And space unfocus, far,
Line, extremity,
Flat and plane a touch
Shiver chill to air.
Nothing helps it much.

Race and waste of blood
Sounds a bell of brass.
Roarings as of flood
Wind the tower, and pass.
As it was decreed
Only circumstance
Knew to help it once.

The endless avalanche
Of silence has its start
Past the pitch of shriek
When nothing hears the heart
And all is quiet within
As the breezes pass
Reciting rotes of grass.
Nothing helps it then.

THE BIRD IN THE THORN

Such lassitude crept on the day
As steals when gales abate;
The air and sky about were gray
And cold as cliffs of slate.

Frozen against the shore of sky
The billowed mountains stood;
A single twisted tree near by
Was proxy for the wood.

And in that tree there sat a bird
In black and ruffled plume
Whose single harsh and raucous word
Queried the courts of doom,

It seemed, of edicts touching sky
And bough and wing and air;
And suddenly I feared reply
Articulated there

To revelation should impeach
Alternatives which hope
Conceives until the act of speech
Give divination shape

As indisputable as stone.
I shouted at the bird.
He lifted, ruffled, at *be gone*
As if he understood.

It was a day when nothing stirred;
Now through all calm I see
The image of that baffled bird
Upon that twisted tree.

THE MANDRAKE

Rich is the reason of the eye;
The time is equinox and noon,
The stalls are stench, and all deny
The mandrake of the chilly moon.

Yet in a sink beneath a hill
As bottomless as day is soon
Lusterless the icon fell,
The mandrake of the chilly moon.

That hollow is a globe devoured
By flutes the blunted withers croon.
The egg was essence, and it flowered
The mandrake of the chilly moon.

SPRING ORCHARDS

Along the roads to Winder
Shrill April airs complain
That mad March blew them kinder;
And orchards bloom again.

On gales the peach is sowing
The blooms it bore in March;
The pear is done with snowing
Its petals white as starch.

Swift busied bees, while plying
The flowering orchards, lift
When sudden flakes go flying
To swell the scented drift

Of petals ebbing Mayward,
Pooling at stick and stone
Until the orchard's wayward
And fragrant storm is blown.

A SPRING SONG

Everywhere
Abroad today
Is the blissful air
That comes with May.

The threadbare earth,
Now May is told,
Is suddenly worth
Its weight in gold;

And the rose's root,
From its bed of gloom,
Through its upthrust shoot
Attains to bloom.

Our spirits weighted
With sorrow's snow
Are half persuaded
They, too, may know,

As winter closes
And days grow fair,
Rewards of roses
To crown despair

And recompense
For all their ills
From the treasury whence
The daffodils.

THE HAYING

To the fields at break of day
The mowers go to cut the hay.

Something is hiding in the green
Field that hates the iron machine.

It hisses so it wakes the hives
Of anger in the sickle's knives.

All day long these war, and make
Sounds like scissors and a snake.

THE THIEF

Time is a thiever of fruit.
Summer has stolen the cherry
From spring, and autumn will loot
Summer of apple and berry:
Time is a thiever of fruit.

TIME AND THE CHERRY TREE

After its early fruit is cast
The cherry tree among its leaves
A gray hour night before and past
Misers the dusk of summer eves;
So there time ever is in error,
The leaves returning light for light
When morning looks into their mirror
While still the boughs lace in the night.

And yet, though time be overtaken
By false resorts among that maze
Of light and shade, one were mistaken
To think it fruit, the ruby blaze
That takes the leaf and sets the bough
Aflame with fall's cheat-cherries now.

At autumn things are all at odds:
From their immortal seeds
Fall to decay the temporal pods;
And over the clairvoyant clods
The blight of winter breeds,
And the world so beautiful.

The year's at a divided way
And may not go but one;
Time that was spring but yesterday
Renews a frosty memory,
And a cold caul dims the sun,
And the world so beautiful.

Summer is shrunken to a wreath
Of holly boughs, alas,
With blood-red berries hung beneath
And thorns sharp as the nettled breath
Grieving as graces pass
From the world so beautiful.

Now while the hale with drunken heads
Hie out under the sky
The ill malinger in their beds
As pain through all their members spreads
And have not strength to die,
And the world so beautiful.

A FIRE OF BOUGHS

At onset of December
When the cold comes to stay
I bring boughs, leafed in May,
To feed the cheerful ember
And warm the wintry night.
Folded into his fur,
The cat disdains to stir
But dreams by firelight.
And I should follow suit
Except that boughs in turning
Shapeless in the burning
Alarms the more than brute
Caged within my being
That often plays at blind
But stirs and shakes my mind
With grave misgiving, seeing
Wood fall from coal to ash,
Its substance burned to nothing,
Its luminescent clothing,
Its shine, its flash,
Expended, one with night—
And is not comforted
That such translation shed
Both warmth and light.

THE FALLEN SNOW

Sorrow and snow are white
The same on a winter's night
That fall, but spheres apart,
On fields and on the heart.

The fallen snow makes strange
A known and narrow range
Where eminences lost
To vision, snow-embossed

Above the whitened plain,
Stand into sight again.
Sorrow and snow fall white
The same on a winter's night.

WINTER SOLSTICE

When the land is white with snow
Something chills the moonlit scene,
Cold so strange no mercury
Apprehends it by degree,
As if feathered fear should go
Like a condor wing between
Heaven and earth; and all of time
Lay defined in whitest rime.
And always the wind comes on to blow.

Let the blackguard wind affright
Fox and owl that wake at night.
Should it rouse a sleeping man
Though it shrink his bones to hear
How it shrills the solstice air
Let him turn to sleep again,
Turn to peace, remembering
That the twice-divided year
Is quartered toward the spring.

III

AS MARY WAS AWALKING
A Carol

I

As Mary was awalking
The budding leaf foreby
The flying fowls were talking
That course the cragged sky

Beneath the roof of thunder
That overtowers the world.
The birds spoke all in wonder
Of finer feathers furled

Than ever shone in plumage
That any bird bedressed.
Maid Mary wore in homage
Those feathers next her breast.

The wing that wore them, beating
The dark of ether, came
To Galilee entreating
The maiden in God's name.

Had any maid soever,
Had any maid so lucked,
Given that angel favor
And not a feather plucked?

As Mary was awalking
When all the leaves were blown
The cattle turned to talking
Apart in undertone:

A maid shall come when winter
Has whited barn and byre.
A stable she shall enter
And birth without a fire

To light Him or to warm Him
The only Son of God.
Lest any seek to harm Him
We horned heads shall nod

While ringed about to greet Him
With welcome of the wold,
And breathe our breath to heat Him
And drive away the cold.

Could any maid soever,
Could any maid so blessed,
Had of the beasts such favor
And not a muzzle kissed?

III

As Mary was awalking
Beneath the wintry boughs
The bare trees fell to talking
In the shadow of Herod's house:

He that shall save the nation,
The Prince of Galilee,
The last appointed station
Shall mount upon a tree.

Men on a cross shall slay Him,
Their Lord shall crucify;
A rood of wood shall stay Him,
Pray God it may be I.

Should mine be chose the timber
To bear God's Holy Son
Though it were then December
I'd all my leaves put on!

Could any maid soever,
Could maiden lent the grace,
Hearken such sweet palaver
And not a bole embrace?

THE GIFTING

There was a giving once of gifts,
And that was done in Bethlehem;
The Magi gifted Mary there
And Mary gifted them.

The three were men of much account,
Each was a king in his own country;
Mary she was a poor lady
And meek and mild was she.

The three came bearing costly gifts,
Each from his treasury could choose;
Mary gave the greatest gift
Of all, no matter whose.

The Wise Men gave three gifts, all told,
Three gifts to Mary's one,
Myrrh and frankincense and gold—
But Mary, Christ her Son!

IN PALESTINE

"What did you see in Palestine?"
"A stable low and a palace fine."
"And what in the stable did you see?"
"The Christ Child in His infancy."
"And what in the palace, little Page?"
"Evil Herod in his age."
"And what was there betwixt the twain?"
"The distance 'twixt the meek and the vain,
  The margin, wider than the sea,
  'Twixt kindness O and cruelty,
  The span so wide no man can tell
  That God has set 'twixt heaven and hell."

IT FELL UPON A WINTER'S MORN

It fell upon a winter's morn
Before the sun arose
When frost was frigid on the corn
And breath steamed in the close

Or I was wakened out of sleep
I drowned into a flood,
And it was twenty centuries deep
And it was Jesus' blood.

I tried to bear my nakedness
Beyond that holy stain,
But not a door would let me pass,
I tried to flee in vain.

When it had risen to my heart
That labored to resign
That blood embraced me every part,
I knew it not from mine.

O I was blood, and of the flow
And crimson flood which swirled
Amongst all men and to and fro
Till washed was all the world.

And when that blood returned again
Which cleansed the world of taint
It entered pure into my vein,
And I awoke, while faint

Bells rang upon the wintry air
And men began to say
And tongues of children to declare
That it was Christmas Day.

THE LITTLE BLIND BOY OF BETHLEHEM

The little blind boy of Bethlehem
Sat on his mother's knee,
And Jesus Christ stood close by them,
That made the blind to see
   To see,
That made the blind to see.

Said He, "What would you have of me
That am the Lord of light?"
"O give the child again to see,
  Like Bartimaeus, sight,
    Sweet Christ,
  Like Bartimaeus, sight."

"I'll give the child again to see
When his dark course is run,
And bright with light that dawn shall be,
Far brighter than the sun
   The sun,
Far brighter than the sun.

"To stave the terror from his way
Until he cop the prize
I give to light his darkened day
Love that sees more than eyes,
    My love, thy love,
Love that sees more than eyes."

The little blind boy of Bethlehem
Long time ago went home.
The light is brighter twice to them
That out of darkness come,
    When into light
The blind from darkness come.

EASTER

Easter is on the field:
Flowers declare
With bloom their tomb unsealed
To April air.

Little lambs
New as the dew shake cold,
Beside their anxious dams:
Easter is on the fold.

AS ONCE A FAMINE WAS ABOUT

As once a famine was about
And pestilence upon the wheat
And men went hungry in and out
And up and down the street,

There came a beggar from the plain
To beg his bread as he was used;
They gave him such a bone of bane
As even the dogs refused.

A lady had a lump of sweet,
She kept it in a covered glass;
It was too precious far to eat.
This lady saw the beggar pass.

She saw he sucked a naked bone
And all the village stared with hate
And God was from their faces gone
That envied him as he ate.

She went among the staring folk,
Her passing turned their tears to drouth;
She broke, as from a shell the yolk,
The sweet into the beggar's mouth.

When she had done with gentle grace
Light on the altered earth revealed
Immanuel in every face
And fruits in every field.

IV

THE SEVEN DAYS OF THE WEEK

I met myself of Monday
At the first strike of the clock;
The more I learned the longer
I listened to it knock.
Except one fail of vision
He may not choose but see,
   And O for a leaf of healing,
   A leaf from that healing tree
   That grows by the river of waters
   That flows by the city of life.

I chid a child of Tuesday
As the sun came up for day
Who shunned the playing children
That circled him in their play.
From his unelected silence
He will never come shouting free,
   And O for a leaf for his healing,
   A leaf from that healing tree
   That grows by the river of waters
   That flows by the city of life.

I glimpsed a girl of Wednesday
As graceful as a gazelle
Fly to the net spread in her way,
And the satyr leap as she fell.
Her pulse throbs to the goat blood
That stirs in her secretly,
   And O for a leaf for her healing,
   A leaf from that healing tree
   That grows by the river of waters
   That flows by the city of life.

I thanked a woman of Thursday
That listened to my suit;
In Frigga's grove grown leafless
That once hung thick with fruit
We labored as devotees
But shall no issue see,
 And O for a leaf for our healing,
 A leaf from that healing tree
  That grows by the river of waters
  That flows by the city of life.

I loved a friend of Friday
As the sun stood up for noon;
Our short and mingled shadows
Were cleft and lengthened soon.
To meet's to part, that fracture
Fissures eternity,
 And O for a leaf for its healing,
 A leaf from that healing tree
  That grows by the river of waters
  That flows by the city of life.

I saw a man of Saturday
Whom the maddening moon had struck;
He stood as gray as the air was gray
At the tag-end of his luck.
His eyes were fixed already
On a country I could not see,
 And O for a leaf for his healing,
 A leaf from that healing tree
  That grows by the river of waters
  That flows by the city of life.

I gazed at a ghost of Sunday
That hangs between two thieves;
His tears flow on His one day,
Yea, seven of seven He grieves
That in the iron heaven
And stone earth even He
    Found not the leaf of healing,
    The leaf of that fabled tree
    That grows by a legend of waters
    That flows through the city of life.

THE POET AND THE VESTURES

Some cloaks came to my mountains,
My beard was three days old,
I gave them drink from the fountains
That flow down candidly cold.
They praised the wine of my mountains,
The water the roots drink from,
And they thought a guitar into my hands
And left me there to strum.
    But I never played a guitar.

They drove to a very great city
Three thousand miles away.
I was there in the city to meet them,
At home there as much as they.
I was shoddily shod, being poor then,
But I looked with the eye of contempt
Upon those empty garments
As rich as mine were unkempt;
Yet I wanted to give them greetings
But what do you say to cloaks?

The vestures had a voice
And memory, I ween;
They said: Now sing for us, Singer,
A song of a mountain scene.
But I sang a song of a city
Planned, placed, perished, gone;
I sang a song of a city
And the city was Babylon.
    Babylon is fallen, is fallen, is fallen.

Then they turned to talking of Sartre
And I to the gilded street
Where they who walk for pleasure
Walk out on candid feet.
In the park near the Colosseum
The bushes hid a brute
That piped a merry music
And stomped a hairy foot.
    That was no guitar he was playing.

I came again to the mountains
And sang my mountain songs
And the words rang clear in Babel
Above the confusion of tongues.
A few were glad at my singing
And lent me an orderly ear,
But most of the men in Babel
Were gabbling too loud to hear
To tin pans, gongs, shrieks and fire alarms.

I have the beard of a mountaineer
But when I am shaven clean
I am John Doe Doakes. In Cleveland
They know what my songs mean.
In Oklahoma City
By true ears they were heard
Though sung through that encumbrance,
A seldom shaven beard.
    A guitar is for a guitar player.

I thought when I heard the music
Played by the merry brute:
There is breath behind that instrument,
It's breath that sounds the flute.

And I was fleeing from Sartre
Whose praiseless praise they sang:
I'll never hang on a coatrack
Though I earn no coat to hang.
  A coat can't play even a guitar.

THE MINSTREL WHO IMAGINED SONG

The minstrel who imagined song
Should buy him bread to eat
Sang to the thoroughfaring throng
At the foot of Tempis Street.
The gawksters gave him guineas none
On which to sup and fare
And when the minstrel's song was done
He had nothing to eat but air,
    And he had plenty of that.

"The song I sang them didn't please,
I'll have to change my tune.
That was winter and death that damped their ease,
I'll sing of Love and June."
And so he sang of love and June
At the foot of Tempis Street.
But after he sang his careless tune
He still had nothing to eat
    But he had plenty of that.

The minstrel stood on the thoroughfare
And said to a passing man,
"What songs do men like best to hear?
I'll sing them if I can."
"Why, men like songs of love and death,
A gay or a sad song."
The minstrel said beneath his breath,
"I must have sung them wrong,
    Wrong from beginning to end."

"Wrong?" said the man on Tempis Street
  Who had an agile ear,
"I thought you sang them right and sweet,
  It moved me much to hear.
You caught no coin into your cap
  Because you're still alive.
You'll have to turn a ghost, my chap,
  The ghosts of minstrels thrive
    That have no need to spend."

The minstrel who imagined song
  Should buy him bread to eat
Sings still to the thoroughfaring throng
  At the foot of Tempis Street.
Since he is dead of an empty craw
  His fortune's on the mend.
    The saddest sight I ever saw
    Was that ghost with coins to spend
    To buy a shift for his bones.

THE LABORING MAN

He that pays the spade respect
Because he's paid it honest salt
Has good reason to reject
The easy ode and hold at fault
The lyric welling lightly up
Without the windlass, as it can.
He likes some blood into his cup;
He bows to none but the laboring man.

God beheld him as he toiled
Because he dreamed His eye in space
To see him tired and see him soiled
And see the worry on his face.
Now when he sings it seems as if
There is nothing easier than
Song; and yet his mind grows stiff
From singing for the laboring man.

Poet of curds and cuff of silk,
Men read the absence of the sun
Upon your countenance of milk.
Return; your labor is not done
Until redone in homespun shirt.
When you have gone and come again
If your hands and heart are hurt
You may sing for the laboring man.

Because it is your grievous fault
To praise the flag and not the staff
Your bed of rose is brined with salt
That else had flowered your epitaph.

He that was shadowed by your sun
Moves from your wake into the van,
And he begins when you are done,
He the doubly laboring man.

THE PERCEPTION OF AGE

When I walked out like a strutting cock
I heard an old man sigh.
Like castanets I heard bones knock
In his flesh as I passed him by.
His flesh, that was silk, had turned as rough
As a hide from the tanner's vat.
(Soon enough, O soon enough
Young flesh comes to that!)
I had no time to stop and talk
And left him soon behind,
But gravely I began to walk
As the old man stalked my mind,
    Slow
        And
           Slow,
As the old man stalked my mind.

When I was searching the looking-glass
For the face in my True-Love's eye
An old man chanced my house to pass,
And I heard the old man sigh.
His pale, parched face was paired with mine
And I was wrung of ease
To tell from the two in the mirror's shine
Which face my True-Love sees;
For now whenever I glance therein
And no one is about
Above an old man's tremble-chin
Two aging eyes look out,
    And out,
Two aging eyes look out.

THE HIATUS

Each nerve is as taut in the body
As a tuned piano wire,
And love is not the culprit
And neither is desire.
You would think a shape so shapeless
As that amorphous sprite
That has stretched the nerves to breaking
Could never cord so tight:
It is nothing at all, it is waiting,
Waiting for it to happen.

Will he manage to meet his appointment
Or miss it by ten per cent?
Will her gown mine memories of Paris,
Dim boulevards by night?
It is not something spoken
Or even thought out straight,
It's a serpent-coil contraction
That tightens while you wait,
While you wait, not ever knowing,
Waiting for it to happen.

The poet cons his pages
And thinks them written right.
His words, if not for ages
May yet endure the night
Obscured with crack-brain clamor
And clanging circumstance.
He speaks them with a stammer
But he must seize his chance.
Melville, dead as a doornail,

Thinks nothing of *Moby Dick*
Since his dark time is not channeled
Through the clock's tick.
Melville is not waiting
For anything to happen.

Stretch your left arm from your shoulder
As far as it will go,
And now your right; untighten
The coil at your center. Though
It is better for only an instant
In that instant dream
You are on the board of directors,
It's a Christian Dior gown,
They think you a second Shakespeare
From Spratford-on-the-James.
Something smiles in silence
At your little games,
Tautening the hiatus
While waiting for it to happen.

A PLATITUDE OF PLATO

Plato sat in the public house
Though he had no right to be there;
He wouldn't tease the barmaids
That played hands through his hair.
He sat like a Grecian statue
And would not suffer the touch
Of the lads like bronze and sunset,
Yet no man loved as much
As Plato loved, as Plato did.

Plato sat on a great stone
Somewhere in the fields of Greece
And the seed that sprang up from the ground
Were only his thought's increase.
He came to a man with a barley hook
And fingered the grain and said:
Because I have thought of the barley seed
It's a better grain for bread.
And no one feasted like Plato,
None feasted as Plato did.

Astride the crack of crisis
With a foot on either side
Plato stood and held his ground
Though the earth was splitting wide.
I am thinking of Good, said Plato
And healed the rifted place.
Of God? asked one with a false ear,
And a smile creased Plato's face,
For no one heard better than Plato,
Heard better than Plato did.

THE LECHERS

The pure pale boys went leching
At sixteen of the clock;
Whenever they saw the shine of flesh
Their knees began to knock.
At lectures or in lobbies
Or where they chanced to stray
They stared the terrible tensions tight
Their hands would ease away
In the nighttime after their daytime
Of innocent lechery.

The pure pale boys went leching;
After the bat had flown
They made a ghostly grinding
Hammering hard on stone.
In the neolithic woodland
Grinding without a sound,
Like primitive Indian women
Squatting upon the ground,
Sat the pure pale boys whose pestles
No softer sink had found.

The pure pale boys went leching
With agitated eyes
Before time took them all in hand
And made them wily and wise
In the ways of casual lovers
That sully in love's flame.
The terror of their noble beasts
Haltering hands touched tame,

But their hearts hammered their ribs hard
Before they learned the game,
The pure pale boys leching
At sixteen of the clock.

I WANDER IN THE AVALANCHE

I wander in the avalanche
That flies before the flail,
And not a blot is apt to blanch
Nor stone be struck to hail

Nor any water, any wind,
Deny it, blood or not,
When night has niggled out the mind
And still the storm is stout.

TO TATTER TOWN

If I went down
To Tatter Town
I'd not go there for hire;
But fetch a face
Or fall embrace
With maniac desire.

The grain that swayed
Before the blade
Is battered into bread;
And yet would I
But thresh it by
And fee the flail instead.

To drunken go
Beneath the bow
And nothing promise it;
But drink the rod
Of gauzing god
And nothing come of it.

(See *Genesis:* IX)

AN EPITAPH FOR ROMANTICS

Lord Byron sat in the boudoir
And stared at the figured walls
While his fancy lady touched her face
Where God had scanted it of grace,
His mind not lofty on a star
Nor yet low as his heels.
 Sing heigh-ho for loving.

Lord Byron swam the Hellespont;
As he swam he cursed at fate—
The which, though atheists think it odd,
Is but another name for God—
That made his foot with a crooked joint
When it might have made it straight.
 Sing heigh-ho for loathing.

Lord Byron crossed the Thracian sea
To give his fevered breath
Fighting for liberty in Greece.
There straightway he won perfect peace;
Yet he that dies for liberty
Is captive then of death.
 Sing heigh-ho for nothing.

THE WAYFARER

The head was never the minstrel
To sing with the heart in the side.
What the heart's soft aye consented
The head's hard nay denied.
But because the heart is stronger
Than the head when one is young,
Head clapped its hands, though feebly,
At what my young heart had sung.
    And the heart was an eager wayfarer
    To the comfortable inn of night.

The head became a preacher,
A fiery evangelist,
And the heart was the song leader
When the sermon was recessed;
But the songs were of a passion
The head had monitored.
The heart then of its own accord
Never sang a word.
    But the heart was still a wayfarer
    To the comfortable inn of night.

Then the head became agnostic,
Not knowing what to believe.
But the heart would not allow the head
To wear it on its sleeve.
For the heart knew of a good thing,
And that good thing was love,
Though the head had no clear inkling
Of the kind the heart knew of.
    And the heart was still a wayfarer
    To the comfortable inn of night.

Between those warring factions
The years have gone like ghosts
Afraid of startling live things,
Slipping from pillar to post.
Still on occasion my heart sings,
But the head is little to me
But a rind grown around silence
Knocking against my knee,
A weight to make me stumble
That else had walked upright
With a young man's tread, though old,
To the comfortable inn of night.

UNDERGROUND

In that subterranean city
To which I came at last
A ghost walked, and was pity,
And the ghost walked past and past.
At the middle bells, at midnight,
Help! cried a bundle of bones.

In that tunnel under the surface
Of light a presence moved,
And that presence had a luminous face
That only the damned have loved.
At the middle bells, at midnight,
O help! cried a bundle of bones.

In that cavern strictly shapen,
Boxed into four-square cells,
A strange thing came to happen
At the sound of the middle bells.
O help! cried the bones at midnight;
Compassion and pity sealed
In that subterranean city
Came, and the bones were healed
At the middle bells, at midnight
In that city underground.

ALWAYS THE WIND

I dreamed of lama wind again
That honed the highlands of Tibet;
Its egret wake was wrung of rain
From which the deserts blossom yet.
And by a pass which none suppose
Its zero shape was flaked to snow
And capped earth's nether ends with floes:
Always the wind comes on to blow.

The passageway which I perceive
Light's length between two rounds of black
Is slacker than an empty sleeve
Except the wind's mouth at the crack
Blow gust by gust to shape it taut
The little distance which we spend
In motion toward the outward ought:
Always and always blows the wind.

Who enter from a torrid tent,
However close and minuscule
The doorway out of darkness rent,
Know well what fan will keep them cool:
The wind that hones the granite rock,
The egret wind, the wind of snow,
The wind that shapes the slackless sock:
Always the wind comes on to blow.

A SIMPLE BY THE SEA

I went down to visit the brewer
That brewed salt in his vat
Filled with the salt sea water
With a fire burning under it.
The water passed off as vapor
And so was purged of its fault
Of spoiling the sea's savor,
And what was left was salt.

A fish moved in the water
With slow, deliberate fin
And looked out at the ragged brewer
That in his turn looked in.
The water that passed as vapor
Seemed the brewer's visible sigh
As he looked into the water
With a fish-like, lidless eye.

I took some salt of his brewing
And sprinkled it into my bread,
And the fish died in the water
And the ragged brewer dropped dead.
The bread changed soon to water
And a vat was formed of the dish,
And I tend the fire in tatters
And stare at the circling fish.

Somebody shall taste of my salt.